THUNDERHEAD

Wisconsin Poetry Series
Edited by Ronald Wallace and Sean Bishop

THUNDERHEAD

EMILY ROSE COLE

The University of Wisconsin Press

Publication of this book has been made possible, in part, through support from the Anonymous Fund of the College of Letters and Science at the University of Wisconsin–Madison.

The University of Wisconsin Press
728 State Street, Suite 443
Madison, Wisconsin 53706
uwpress.wisc.edu

Gray's Inn House, 127 Clerkenwell Road
London EC1R 5DB, United Kingdom
eurospanbookstore.com

Printed in the United States of America
This book may be available in a digital edition.

Library of Congress Cataloging-in-Publication Data
Names: Cole, Emily Rose, author.
Title: Thunderhead / Emily Rose Cole.
Description: Madison, Wisconsin : The University of Wisconsin
    Press, [2022] | Series: Wisconsin poetry series
Identifiers: LCCN 2021041583 | ISBN 9780299336745
    (paperback)
Subjects: LCSH: Daughters—Poetry. | LCGFT: Poetry.
Classification: LCC PS3603.O42828 T49 2022 |
    DDC 811/.6—dc23

LC record available at https://lccn.loc.gov/2021041583

For every daughter

CONTENTS

PART THREE

THUNDERHEAD

SELF-PORTRAIT AS JUDY GARLAND

When I was three, my mother caught a bluebird
and stitched her into my throat while I slept, seam

of sinew sewn to wing. Blood pooled into my pillow.
I woke with feathers shot through the sticky ropes of my hair.

At first, I had trouble swallowing, but I learned to gulp
around the beating-hearted bulge beneath my chin.

When she sang, I turned mockingbird, mimicking
her muffled trills, the blue croon of her warbling.

At thirteen, I took off: landed job after job, chased
Benzedrine with Hershey's Kisses. On nights blurred

salty by vodka and sleeping pills, we'd hum lullabies
in A-minor and I'd finger the scars threaded to my neck,

the ones that held her inside me. At sixteen, I crammed my toes
into a pair of spangled silver heels, threw the deadbolt

across my trailer door. I pried those careful stitches out
with a rust-edged steak knife, stained my shoes red

as she surged from my mouth, wings oiled in blood,
song bright as polished tin. She was gone

when they found me, escaped out a back window.
She left me with scratches on my cheeks, a throat

full of feathers, and my own precious, blue voice.

I

Are you a good witch or a bad witch?

FRANK L. BAUM

SPELL FOR THE FISSURED BRAIN

Only edged things. Lemon-mint, locust husks, a peach pit sucked of flesh. Nothing lucky, loved, or mystical: everything ordinary & small enough to fit in the first fold of a girl's skirt. Here's the hard part: wait for a lightningless storm. Don't expect, but prepare: pleat the ingredients into hems, pockets, fists. Fix an eye, always, on the bulleting clouds. When they rupture, trust your hands, their sturdiness. Watch. In your bowled palms, those common things will glimmer. Will overrun. Will rise.

DOUBLE MEMORY WITH TRAIN

Once, Mama cradled my head to her chest
and told me how she spread loose change

on the tracks that cut so close beside her house,
the dishes shook when trains bellowed in.
She'd crush her belly to the yellow throats

of onion grass and tuck her chin as weight
and wheels pressed her pennies to palm-flat smears.

I think she knew, even then,
how absence freights the memory:
her father's chair empty at dinner,

his stethoscope always poised
over someone else's heart.

In the memory I make for her, she leaps
from rail to rail, pockets clattering
with beaten copper. He waits for her

in the kitchen, hands open
to collect her bounty of ruin.

IMAGINED SNAPSHOT

Morningstar Studios, 1988

Somewhere, the picture must exist, or at least
I want it to: her hand ambling up the neck
of her Martin, her eyes half-lidded

(just like mine when I'm singing),
the crowshine of her untrained alto
almost a tangible glimmer, like the flash
at the edge of the glass. Behind her,

the walls bulge black with sound-catching
foam. The microphone she's lilting into costs
more than her car. Even music has a cost.

For now, my father, out of frame, hammering
the thick strings of his dulcimer, is happy
to pay it. He doesn't know I'm there—

spare cluster of cells, small pearl of not-yet
bone. In eight months, I'll have a finch-

feathered voice like hers
and not like hers. In twelve years,
he'll be bringing me here

instead. I want to preserve her
joy, preserve her not knowing
that she's growing her own

replacement, that the band won't split
when my parents do, that this

is the last song she'll ever record.

LENT

In this season when sugar turns ash,
Mama and I rise before school
to buy fasnachts, buttery lumps
of potato flour, from the best bakery in town.

I wear ChapStick to trap sugar on my lips,
to hide between my teeth this metaphor
for everything I'll lose in Lent,
this promise:
                          what I love can leave me.

I know no matter how many prayers I hurl
into heaven, I can't take back the kiss seared
on Jesus' brow, the bread of his bones.
I can't save Mama from mourning,

and so, as always, her love will wither like a bulb
buried too close to winter, will vanish as surely as hallelujahs
from our mouths. No praise now, because Lent
is the wrong season for joy.

I know better than to test her, but I do it
anyway, holler *hallelujah* when the sky spits snow,
wide flakes that'll turn to rain that night.

She grinds her teeth and doesn't speak to me
until dinner: *Jesus*, she prays, *make us sorry
for our sins, offer us the grace to repent.*
We sing hymns until long after bedtime—

                     let all mortal flesh keep silent,
                     ponder nothing earthly minded—

and I'm almost sorry.
But the next day, soot-cross darkening
my forehead, I bless everything
on the playground: worms scooped

from the sidewalk return alive
to the soaked earth, *hallelujah*,
only two girls murmur *freak* and point at me,
hallelujah, when a ball whistles from a boy's hand

it misses me, *hallelujah*,
my teacher lets me stay inside for the rest of recess
and I fill the empty chalkboard, the tail
of each *a* like the tongue of a lily:

hallelujah, hallelujah, hallelujah.

These blessings, not for me, not for them,
but for Mama—as if blessing something
is the same as fixing it. As if enough

forbidden praise could drag Jesus back
before he leaves us, leaves her, alone
and wanting what I can never give her,
some other love than mine.

SELF-PORTRAIT AS RAPUNZEL

i.

Mama built her tower out of baby teeth
broken on stale communion wafers, out of dogs

choked by chicken bones, empty medicine cabinets,
every lullaby her mother never sang her.

When I was born, she mixed a mortar of bent
needles, busted harp strings, and porcupine
quills pulled from beneath her fingernails.

One day, she told me, *gold dust will pool in the hollow
of your tongue. Roses will track their roots in your spine.
Your body will chip like shale rock chiseled by rain.*

ii.

She shut me in. No door. One locked window.
A keyhole cut in the shape of my name.

I stayed inside for years, afraid of anything
that carried its shadow too close to itself.
Mama hoisted baskets of mint and dill.

She wrote notes that ended with *for your own good*
and planted morning glories that opened like eyes.

iii.

When a prince arrived, he used words like *trapped*
and *escape*. I offered a rope woven from daisy stems,
but he said my hair was stronger.

The shorn end of the braid thumped the grass
like a feathered body striking stones. Years later,
after he left me, I carved a hole in my tongue.

I came home. The tower had fallen. Mama's last gift:
a handful of pebbles shaping a word: *grow*.

I built my tower out of nettles and closed doors,
and dropped seeds into my eyes.

iv.

Now, red petals curl behind my teeth.
Pollen smears my lips and bees
drone at the corners of my mouth.

I swallow secrets that harden into keys.
All night, I listen to locks sliding shut.

LOVEBITES

The dog wiggles onto my chest, gums humming
the music of *bite*. She's just a puppy, so it's cute
when she clutches her jaws to the crest of my nose.

At least, Mama thinks so. *Lovebites*, she says,
as if the spaniel's need to chew would dull the reek
of her breath or ease the stitches of red I'll dash
with concealer before school tomorrow morning.
As if *bite* were inextricable from *love*. We both

grew up like that, Mama and I, thinking love
isn't love unless it draws blood—just like a dog
bite, so warm, so full of bright, bright teeth.

PRAYER

Crouched between the mower, its oilcan
and the tree that just missed the van Gogh
Daddy loved (but not enough to take it

with him), warm musk of sawdust itching
my nostrils, I strike the match head hard
against the trestle of his work bench and light

the wild sage smuggled from a garden
that is not Mama's. I remember the story
she told me once, about the time she

and her friends played with a spirit
board. How one girl's fingers quaked
around the planchette like a startled bird,

how her eyes rolled, lidless, into white,
how her voice flapped like a loose hasp
against a barn door, hissing *yes yes yes*.

If Mama finds me here, drawing rough symbols
with a burnt bundle of leaves, she'll whet
the edges of her mouth and wring me back

through the hem of mud and high grass,
up to my room, where she'll bend
my knees like a lash and buckle her fingers

over mine as I ask for deliverance
from evil. The sage smoke smells white
and clean. I whisper the spell I learned

at the library when no one was looking and hope
I'm asking the right gods for protection.
I hope there are gods to ask.

I am nine years old.

There is nothing to believe in
but magic.

IN THE YEAR OF THE DIVORCE, MY FASCINATIONS INCLUDE: SURREALISM, THE DUST BOWL, AND *THE WIZARD OF OZ*

That night, a high wind whipped grit at our windows, drowned
the radio. When Daddy's eyes rolled out of his sockets,
he caught one in the notched cup of his palm.

Mama chased the other through our battened shack, wrestled
it away from our thin-boned cat. These things happen:

twisters split the roots of our foundation, rust tatters
the edges of our spoons, the bell of every bowl is weighted
with dust. When she offered him his eye, smut-black and oozing,

he closed the other into her hand, said, *Cook 'em.*
Let's eat real meat tonight.

The next day, Daddy woke with spiders nesting
where his eyes used to be. He cleared the cobwebs

with a swept thumb and sent me to melt down all Mama's
thimbles. When they cooled to balls, he told me to paint them

blue, like he always wanted. They didn't plug the holes
quite right, one false eye lolling like our back door loosed
from half its hinges. Metal leaked into his blood.

Now, his tongue's feathered with rust. He spits pennies
instead of tobacco. He and Mama don't talk. All night, we hear
him scraping his teeth against the wet smile of his axe.

Daddy's changed. Stripe rust thickens on the wheat
and his breath reddens the dust. He still sees me

a little, but I don't think he sees Mama anymore.
She fixes him lunches of screws and banjo strings.

He never thanks her. Once, I saw her juice a plum
into the bowl, rust shut his jaw. When I oiled it open,

he dropped all Mama's needles down his throat and said
he'd spit them back at her, said he'd aim for the eyes.

When the next storm seethed through, she shoved him
into the rain and jimmied open his chest, found a cluster
of dynamite where his heart should be.

I watched from behind the kitchen door. She said,
I've had enough, and cut the bundle loose with her last

pair of sewing scissors. He took it out into the barn,
his heart in one hand, his axe in the other.

The day he left, Daddy twisted a nut around each
of my small fingers. *Now your hands will shine.*

That night, I shrieked awake:
steel girdled my skin, all that shine swallowed up
in blood, metal rings notched snug under my knuckles.

When Mama came, it was too late
to cut them out, too late to do anything
but rock her hands over mine and teach me
how to bind my split-up fingers into fists.

PROTECTION SPELL

Only purpled things. Skullcap, milk thistle, columbine
bludgeoned with a pestle. Nothing you would call
talisman, nothing that, if taken from you, could
be recognized for its magic. Split cork, seaglass,
left wing of a luna moth. Bind them over a pulse
point: wrist, breast, jugular. Trust your blood to
stir their power. It's blood that makes the bruise.

SOMEWHERE BRIGHTER

Mama didn't hit me much.

        I remember, most clearly,
    a day when I was seven. She'd raked all morning,
        hefted a bag fat with leaves,

and when I called from my perch
    in a low tree, she did as I asked, opened it
for me to jump into.

        But when courage fled me and I clung
           to my branch, made her wait too long
in the sun, she reddened my cheeks
        with an open palm. *Coward*, she hissed,
hoisting the sack to her shoulder.
           That's for wasting my time. Since then,

every story I love begins like this: *Once upon a time*

    there was a girl   *and she was brave.*

No surprise I chose Dorothy for my favorite,
        bright champion in her shined-up shoes,
    and her bluebird voice,
        so much like mine,

who faced the world as if she weren't afraid
        of anything—not lions, not forests
    dark with witches, or men
        with faces made of fire.

She wasn't scared to run from home
           or back to it.

That Christmas I asked for nothing
                  but a checkered dress, red shoes,
        two ribbons to knot loose
              at the ends of my braids.

        Is it wrong to say these tokens
    didn't make me less afraid?

        When, for example, a sliver from the deck
    bit beneath my pinky nail,
            I couldn't fake Dorothy's calm.
    I wailed into Mama's arms, sniffled
as she, head nurse for ten years at Jesus camp,
            lifted down her kit from the bathroom cabinet,
        stroked her thumb over my cheek
                as she showed me the scalpel's long, shining tooth.

She promised *I won't hurt you*
            and grazed the flat of the blade over my skin,
    murmuring *hush now, click your heels.*

            I'd grown out of those shoes by the time
    I reached for that scalpel on my own.

Mama had gone out somewhere
            when a storm gnarred down
                from its mottled thatch of thunderheads—
tornado warning.

        Fourteen now and still my stupid fingers
    shook too hard to strike
                a match when the power went out.

No candles and no knowing
where the flashlights were, but the blade lit
up like a beacon when lightning
                    gnashed its snaggled teeth.

        I don't have a good answer
for why I chose that day to begin
                    the ritual of slicing a shallow smirk
    into my ankle—just enough
            to shriek the nerves, to dribble blood—
except that it was punishment
        for being too afraid to call Mama
    and ask her to come home.

        Punishment for preferring to wait in the dark
    while oaks battered the windows
                    than to risk her coming back to rage
    about the flooded basement.

        Punishment because, before I reached
for the bandage she'd never notice,
    I smeared my thumb
            over the white of my sneakers
and tapped them together,
                    asked for the house to uproot,
        for the storm to spin me
            somewhere brighter than here,
somewhere with no gold road
            to lead me back.

MEDITATION WITH INFINITY

Zero is a number in the way that Christ was a man.
EULA BISS

When I was a child, it didn't seem so impossible, the end
and the end looped elegantly together—an eternal devouring,
my pink-mouthed kitten never catching her tail. I used infinity
the way most children do: an unequaled argument-killer,
I'm right, infinity. I'm bad with numbers and never got why
the rejoinder, *infinity plus one*, couldn't exist. Pure concepts
elude me. But even then I understood infinity as a number high
enough to become incomprehensible. Like heaven. Like love—

I told my mother once, *I love you infinity*, and she chided me
that this was impossible. *When I was a child, I thought like a child,*
reasoned like a child. From the Mamertine prison, the apostle
Paul wrote my favorite three words in the Bible: *Love never fails.*
Mama, is *never* as impossible as infinity, or just imaginary?
I knew failure like I knew my penknife's accidental slit in my
fingers, its irreversible cicatrix, but I needed to believe that even
then, love remains somehow infinite—a closed loop, a number
as inscrutable, as unbelievable, as zero.

FOUR POISONS

i.

Even after frost, that clutch of pokeweed leers
from a gutted bush as I walk by, fruit thick
as a boy's jawbone on the waning vine.

I'd like to pulp them under the heels
of my hands, drip poison through the faults
lined in my palms. When my dad dropped

like a rotted apple and rolled to another town,
I stared all summer at those dark berries skeining
what used to be his toolshed.

I wanted to sleep with my tongue
the same purple as the veins
in Mama's neck when she told him,
*You will give me your respect and so
will your ingrate daughter.*

I wanted to eat. I wanted to hurt.

ii.

My college roommate and I discuss how best to slip
our parents their meds. I tell her about crushing

lithium into Mama's homemade applesauce, still pink
with peel. When I call her for the first time in a month,

she tells me she lost her job—no more pills, no more health
insurance—so I say, *I won't be home for Christmas*

this year. She'll be happier without me.
She says, *Your first word should have been "abandon."*

iii.

In middle school, I ink lists of black-eyed things
on the hinge of my right wrist: peas and Susans,

> a dead wren cleaved with maggots, the girl who sits
> beside me in homeroom with her shuttered face
> pale as Xanax, no makeup on the blue-black ring
> my dad once called *a shiner.*

One day, I touch her wrist and whisper, *You're lucky.*
At least they're leaving you something that'll heal.
A hurt you can prove if you have to.

Forgive me, black-eyed girl.
I thought I was telling the truth.

iv.

The first time I meet my girlfriend, it's past midnight.
She flattens her teeth to my throat, my back to the door.

> I say, *Let's count the flares from the gas wells.*
> *There's a place where the groundwater burns.*
> *Let's find it. Let's take a candle and a match.*

She says, *I love you like a field full of jasmine.*

> I don't say, *No one could love a girl like me.*
> *My heart is a shipwreck of ice.*

> *Every word I know rhymes with "abandon."*

PREMONITION

That summer, the mimosa tree sickened and dropped
a shroud of wilted crowns over my father's backyard.

This was before the rain garden dug its purple thumbprint
of foxglove and thistle into the landscape, before the deer
bloodied their mouths with the last of our raspberries, before

mother and *cancer* rattled from my mouth on the same breath.

Even when the back deck was just an outline of postholes
and chalk, my father still hung his feeder from the dying tree
to tempt nuthatches and tanagers and the red-bellied woodpecker

that shelled sunflower seeds in the long cinch of his beak.
I had just stepped from the shower when my father pounded
on the bathroom door: *come look, come quick.* Sheathed

in a bath towel, I hurried to the kitchen, saw him point
out the glass door at the hawk, the scattering sparrows.

Talons clinched in the woodpecker's breast, red and deeper
red. There was not much struggle. The long mouth gawped
as the hawk yanked feathers from its neck, plucked it alive.
A thin moan hacked from its throat.
                                        Its eyes were open.

I would like to tell you that I squeezed my lip between my teeth
and listened to my father when he said it was *a natural cycle.*

I was sixteen, and I thought I knew everything, thought I understood
death. I would like to tell you that I looked back at the doomed bird
and did not see the buttons of my mother's favorite jacket

stamped on its clouded eyes. I would like to tell you anything
but that, half-naked and trembling, I ran back to the bathroom

to disappear in a cloud of steam. Anything but that, four years

later, when my mother called and said *hospice*,
I knew, already, exactly what would happen.

II

At the end of my suffering
There was a door.
LOUISE GLÜCK

SPELL FOR COURAGE

Only crushed things. Spider legs, sassafras twigs, a rat's skull unburied from your garden. No feathers, not even broken ones. No hints at flight. Instead: two sprigs of thyme mashed between your teeth. You are more afraid of naked light than of darkness, so cast at noon, under open sky. Leave the matchbox in its drawer. You will not need to burn anything, but you will want to. What you crushed, give to the wind. In place of an incantation, unstitch the secret sewn to the underside of your tongue. You know the one. Say it. Say it again.

SELF-PORTRAIT AS PERSEPHONE RETURNING

This before everything: shame.
I disappeared, so she fettered the earth

with snow. She tried to drag Hell
to her doorstep: everything dead—
cattle fallen in the frost-wrecked fields,
the choked river's familiar moan,
icicles spearing the trees. What did I expect?

To leave a hemorrhage
of violets wherever I walked?

No. A lost son is called *prodigal*.
A lost daughter is just called *lost*.

PASSPORT

Like a spoon scritching the bottom of a tin bowl, Mama's voice
scrapes through the phone, saying *transplant*, saying *30 percent chance.*

Spring comes late to northern Pennsylvania, the heads of trout lilies
bent with the last smattering of snow. Chickadees chatter in the crook

of a magnolia that won't bloom for two more weeks, but still I return
to it, praying the gray pods will have broken overnight.

I know what questions to ask, the language of cancer lodged
in my mouth like a rotted tooth, but I say instead,

My visa came today, tell her about my unsmiling photo,
how the seal shimmers and reads "étudiante."

I could stay, I tell Mama, because I have to—
because good daughters always say *yes.*

I say, *I could give you my marrow* and mean,
I could give you my year in Toulouse. Take it.

Take the chocolate heart spun in the center a croissant,
take the Basilique Saint-Sernin's hourly racket of bells,

take the peacock feather from the Jardin des Plantes,
where roses reach full bloom by mid-February.

In the pause that follows, I wish there were leaves
for the wind to tremble through instead of just my scarf,

its tassels twirling, as if for joy.
You're not the right blood type, she tells me. *Don't stay.*

I don't know whether to say *thank you* or *I'm sorry* so I settle for
I love you, and she says she loves me too, says *I'll let you go now.*

ANOTHER PREMONITION

The south wind scrabbles   down brick-stitched streets

        strewing Place du Capitole with ashtrays

    snatched shawls

                    a child's lost umbrella

      & rears the crumpled ivy into whips

claws through slatted shutters to champ
                its hard gray mouth against the back

of my neck to wrench   me from a dream of my dead-

       eyed mother shrieking

          as a biopsy needle burrows
    marrow-deep into her hipbone &

      I judder like a door blown open

PORTRAIT

Mama as Demeter

Everything is about loss. The bees, too long overwintered, still beat
double-time to preserve their queen. I would take them

as I've taken everything else—the hawk's eyes eaten,
the farmer's toenails curled in death, his wife's greasy lip-
print on his whiskey glass—except you always loved bees
and I wanted you not to have them
down there with you.

I am kind. I don't keep the lake from rifting.
Beneath the weakening ice, a flounder's scales
yellow back to life. Soon you, too,
will unfreeze. Yes, daughter. I do want

you back. My laudanum. My satellite. Buried seed
pearl, mine. But can't I love this deprivation
a little longer? There is joy

in taking. Even from you.

HER CANCER INTO HARVEST

Sixteen again, Mama's hair is sunshot as the wheat

she wades through—stems part like arms bent back.

She circle-sweeps the sickle with the ease of a heron's wing

cleaving the rippled skin of a lake, scythes seeds

into the wide bowl she holds in a crooked arm.

The jagged stalks blacken, sharpen to arrowheads

that split her palms down their lifelines. Skinless

hands rise up from the earth, break open the topsoil.

Their razored fingers slit the muscles loose around her wrists,

her ankles. Her bowl expands: she topples in, laid on a bed of chaff.

Those hands rear back, toss her. She separates. Wind yanks out

her hair in clumps. Plumes of blood billow like prayer flags

and her tasseled voice lifts over the dead field:

From the teeth of my mouth may God

grow a grove of blood oranges.

I want this to be a dream—those hands, those knives

of wheat. The hospital doors hiss apart and I hear

in the shallow bowl the clack of winnowed bone.

STILL LIFE WITH LINES FROM ISAIAH

This morning Mama rasped *go to hell* but I stay balled
between these machines and their racket of artifice.

I don't know how she sleeps through it. False breath.
Heart skips. I'm afraid to unhitch the rosary from her fingers,
so I thumb open her Bible instead. I want the needle

thirsting in her wrist to tell her, *Fear not for I am
with you.* It's late July and the windows won't open.
Sweat daubs the backs of my knees. Levaquin drips

from its jangle of tubes and I imagine the mouth
of each doctor shaping the word *dismay.* Her bed,
from this angle, looks like an altar. Isaiah, when you wrote,

The wolf will live with the lamb, what did you mean?
Some days, cancer is the wolf. Some days, the wolf is Mama.

SNAPDRAGONS (I)

In the year of the wig & the blood bank, I brought sheaves
of snapdragons to brighten Mama's window, nested them
between her untouched breakfast & the statue of Jesus
shouldering a lamb. I wanted them to guard her, these gold-
necked spitfires she pinched open, fingers clumsy with nausea,
as I recited Psalm 23 so their gaping wouldn't look like a scream.
I wanted them tongued & clawed. I wanted them snapping
the biopsy needle in two. I wanted it not to be too late.

AFTER THE TRANSPLANT FAILS, I DREAM OF CROCODILES

strutting under Grandma's kitchen table,

fangs shaped like candle flares
          perched on white linen. The old clock

clips time with the tails
          that knock over her rosewood chairs.

Grandma swears we're safe with a shut door—
          We just don't go in there anymore sweetheart,

but the water leaking through the hinges
          unnerves me. She says it's God

who put them there, *a test of will*, but
          I can only think of Sobek, leather-snouted master

of the Nile, whose children were crocodiles.
          The Egyptians drowned their votives in the river:

figurines and amulets, vessels with an offering
          drawn from a vein—*Sobek, protect us, smite*

our enemies. Strange, that a god of war
          would carry his young between his jaws.

Maybe it's a matter of sacrifice. Don't all gods
          require this unzipping of flesh, this kindle

of bone? I've given Grandma's God
          the crumpled cusp

of my neck, spent knees, my body—a temple
        swept clean of pleasure. I stand naked

at the kitchen door, blood slathering my cheeks,
        a rough crown of flies at my ears.

Claws roil the water, scaled bellies slap
        the floor. I click back the lock to wade over the carpet.

When I wake, I'm in my aunt's old bed.
        Grandma's kitchen is empty.

I know this. But I think, *My mother is dying*
        in the next room, and God has given me nothing

but crocodiles. Outside, the moon sickles the night,
        its bales of light dissolving in an oak's ragged teeth.

HOSPICE

Mama has been four days at Saint Luke's, her color still
good. I sign in each day before nine—brought by my
Grandpa, or Mama's new husband—and pour coffee I
forget to drink. She eats what we bring her, sometimes
takes visitors. Today, an old bandmate helps her choose
music for her memorial. When he teaches me the second
part of a reworked hymn, my harmony splinters and
breaks. She says she hopes I'll practice. The next day, I sing
to bury a hook in the roof of her mouth. I sing to leaven her
blood. I sing to yank her back. When I close my mouth, she
turns to her husband, says, *I'd like calla lilies at the altar.*

ALL I WANTED

We counted crocuses on the way to school,
white and purple eyelids blinking between roots
of ice, my small hand thin as smoke in your grip.

We counted them in pairs and triads and strangled
single shoots. Six was the turning point, you'd say,

six was proof the earth could still breathe
through the black frost in its lungs. Late March,

my birthday looming, and all I wanted
was for spring to seep back into your skin.

Oh Mama, forgive me. How could I have known,

the week before your transplant, when I snapped
a picture of a clutch of six crocuses, their yellow
lashes uncurled against a sheet of snow,

that you'd keep the whole ICU awake, screaming,
afraid you'd never see even one of them again?

Months later, when the marrow
you borrowed from your brother turned

on you, the only thing blooming in the hospice
garden was a strand of irises latched
beneath your window. Six of them.

One for each day you lived.

Mama, here is what I never told you:
That last morning, I wrenched open
their blue and purple throats,

snatched out their palsied tongues,
ground them under my muddy boots.

NOCTURNE WITH WITCH & DESIRE

Dear black-furred night dripping
star-shear, dear moon shucking eggs
down the thighs of a million ravenous
unmothers, give me a clutch of women to eat

like strawberries. Give me their spark plugs
to swallow, their hard breath motorcycling up
my wrists. Give me a spur of jasmine pinked
with gore to diadem my head, give me a head
for wanting, give me a heart-mouthed conch, a river
of unclosed legs, a desire that isn't punitive, give it
over, give it up, give it all to me because I desire
it. Give it because I asked. Just because I asked.

MRI, BARNES JEWISH HOSPITAL

This is the second time I've lain on my back and thought *corpse.*

The optometrist says, *atrophy,*
the neurologist answers, *lesions.*

My brain riddled with questions.

This is the second time and I am not less afraid.

In pictures, Lucia, patron saint of blindness,
carries her eyes on a silver tray. Starting at six,

I dressed like her every year for her Saint's Day,
awake before the birds, my grandpa said, before

the grownups, to bring them breakfast,
my sash's dribble of red interrupting the white

of my slip-dress, tray weighted with *lussekatter*
instead of irises. But I knew the story,

and even then I understood why a girl would take
her own eyes out so a man wouldn't want her.

                    I wonder now if they looked like mine.

I don't know how to tell you what this sounds like.
I'm trying. When the technicians hung headphones

over my ears and asked me to pick a radio station
to cover the noise, I said, *No. I'm a poet, I want to listen.*

(This impressed them. Afterward, I gave
a brief lecture on how to catch girls

with sonnets.) Now, my imagination strains:
A choir of lionesses? A woodchipper
                                                    swallowing an arm of birch?

None of this is right.

✦

Have I said Lucia wears a wreath of candles?
I was never sure why. In Sweden, there's a story
of a winter famine broken by a girl crowned in light
and fixed at the helm of a ship loaded with grain.

Or maybe it's just that her name means light. Her day
falls on the solstice, *the coldest, darkest night*,
Mama told me before bed. *That far north, the nights
are so long you don't know if you'll live through them.*

After she'd gone, I switched my own electric crown
on and off to watch the cheap bulbs spark and hum.

✦

Before they put me in here,
         the phlebotomist asked
                  if I had good veins

and I didn't consider what *good* meant
         before I said *yes.*
                  Now, I think of Mama, try to count

how many transfusions she needed.
         I am not supposed to move,
                  but as this machine lifts

its many voices, my mouth
         shapes that familiar mantra,

                  not cancer, not cancer.

✦

Dear Lucia   this machine rumbles with light
                                      and still I am afraid

something is wrong with my eyes   Lucia

         like a snagged hem
                           my optic nerves unravel

         they can't fix it   Lucia   can I confess to you
                  can I confess   I am neither brave
                                            nor pious

but teach me   Lucia

                                  to be blind

✦

When I shuffled down the stairs that morning,
I put the wreath on first, let it lead me through

our shadowed house as I poured coffee and stacked
saffron buns. I didn't care if it was crooked

between my tattered braids, the tangle
of evergreen sprigs scraping my ears,
                              one bulb dead

as I hefted my platter. I didn't care.
This crown carried light in it, so I rose

up the stairs like a saint,
believing that even a blind girl

              could break the neck of the dark.

III

We must admit there will be music despite everything.

JACK GILBERT

SPELL FOR THE GRIEF SONG SCARRED TO YOUR THROAT

Only riven things. Milkweed pod, trampled jonquil,
twinned halves of a wren's wrenched egg. Resist tracing
their breakages with a hungry thumb. Go, alone, to the
closest river & kneel where the bank is softest. Don't sing.
Dig. Loose the soil, arms heavy with dirt as they lower.
Give back everything clefted, schismed. Incantation:
I miss you. Unearth your heart, jarred & embalmed
in cinnamon. It's still yours. Hold it. Take it home.

AT HER FUNERAL, SINGING

pie Jesu   you take

      .& take

the garnet   she would have

      given me

        red drop   mis-

     shapen cell   *dona eis*

requiem   which sins

    Domine   are mine

are hers *pie*
       Jesu

        whose voice

     plummeting

WHAT MAKES A PEARL

When she died, I took my mother's socks,
those fuzzy polka-dotted ones she'd worn
in hospice. I wore them all through winter.

Maybe that's creepy. But is it really so different
from the necklace she willed to me,

that single pearl clinging to its strand of silver?

The necklace isn't creepy. Every day for a year
I hung it over my heart, even in the shower,
even when it felt heavy as a beggar's first coin.

I want to say that having these talismans is like having a scar,
but worse. That, in winter, socks are as inevitable as scars,

except there's more choice in it: when I'm cold,
I choose which socks to wear, and whose.

But I know now, after washing them to near-
translucence, that these tokens I harvested
from Mama's deathbed are more like the pearl,

or rather, what makes a pearl:
that piece of sand, the irritant that the nacre
builds itself around, that tiny, everyday object

that, little by little, learns to glow.

ELEGY WITH HEMLOCK & COLD TEA

For days after the funeral   I left fresh mugs
of oolong everywhere   the bathroom sink
a countertop   my dad's new hardwood floor

He never grumbled at me as he wiped
the dark rings up   let me indulge
in grief's long rituals of forgetting

I never finished more than half a cup
while it was still hot   & when   as we left
to box her things   I found a cold   third-

drunk latte in my stepfather's car
he confessed that he kept trying
to self-soothe with Starbucks but failed

to drink any before it cooled   Only then
for the first time in the three years I'd
known him   did I understand that we

had in common something more
than my mother   more than the grand
scheme of our mourning   that we shared

these recurrent little calamities of finding
something tepid that we had wanted
warm   We understood   both of us

how grief settles in the root
of a stomach like fine sediment   How
its circle warps the grain of a life

We're like a pair of eastern hemlocks   He
& I   perhaps if someone axed us
down   we'd expose the same number

of rings that Mama grooved in us   nine
now   almost a decade of circular sorrow
a stain   neither of us can scour

SELF-PORTRAIT AS DOROTHY GALE

These days, my bones are thrush-thin and all I want
is a winnowing. I want skin loosening at the small
of my back, wind lifting me like an exaltation

of ragweed. What a blessing, to be carried
like a child in a womb. My mother fell asleep
in the earth and now I'm as still as a beating heart.

I sleep in my truckbed, keep the radio tuned
to the weather. No place feels like home.

Soon another storm will kick its heels
in my face—gunmetal clouds closing
into thunderheads, pines hurling down

their sap-ripe ribs. I enter the field alone,
rain lashing my eyelids shut, scarecrow
my arms, and speak to the cyclone like a mare
I used to ride when I was young.

I tell it, *I don't want to be here.*
I tell it, *We are the same kind of runaway.*

I tell it, *Take me back.*

LOVE POEM TO RISK

You move over my chest like the swab

of iodine before the scalpel. You're the fourth
shot of whiskey at a party I leave too late, the heels

I wear walking home after dark, and the man
watching me from the other side of the street.

When I was thirteen, you made me pack a go-bag—
toothbrush, Walkman, second-favorite dress,

a scrawled note for my mother—*I'm better off
gone*. You're the reason I can leave anywhere

in under five minutes, a carry-on always stashed
under the bed. But I've never stopped seeing you

for what you are: the siren's stuttering keen
and the storm cellar's loose hinges,

both the lightning that doesn't feather
my arm and the charred ground beside me.

You touch your teeth to my pulse
and claim nothing good happens without you.

I still can't say you're wrong.

IN TOULOUSE (I)

After the burial   white ash
      clay pot

    my tongue heavy as stone
        I return

   to this land whose language lacks

          a word for *home*

this city whose name I always
       want to write
        to lose

   In the park I watch the wind

       crumple a small girl's kite
under Pont Neuf's center arch

   She wails

      & the wind wails back

& I wish it would take me too

      pitch me up to join this carillon

this terror of mourning

MS NOCTURNE WITHOUT A MAGICIAN

Night of hacksaw wind & tick-fat moon, of dog groan & failed
medication, night I'm filling with letters to the body I can't sleep in:

Dear body,   get your shit together because if we keep going
to the bathroom this much, we'll never sleep more than an hour

at a time. Dear body,   let there be another way out of this
than through the chute of a syringe wasping in our thigh.

Tell me that this year is the first half of a magic trick,
the part when the woman's severed feet

dangle from one box & across the stage her head
simpers from another.   Tell me that any minute

some magician will stroll in to drop a curtain,
waggle his fingers, then—*ta-da!*—we'll be made

whole, each chasm in our brain erased.
Dear body,   how do I begin to love you again?

Teach me to stop trying
to resurrect what is already alive.

AT CIMETIÈRE DE TERRE CABADE

I walk in the shadow of headstones pocked
with mums and white violets, a lone sunflower.

In France, all the cities close for the dead.
No school, no bread, no early grapes

from the outdoor market. It's *Toussaint*,
twelve days after I left you

in the ground back in Pennsylvania,
and the graveyards are littered

with eyes—a cat growling
through the scrub, that daisy wrecked

with worms, ripped leaves trembling
under my bootheels. The air is thick

with ghosts, Mama, and I wonder
if you miss me. Lacing my arms

through an angel's, I swing onto a grave,
flowers falling at my feet, to cup

a cherub's cheek. Its eyes gawp
back at me, and Mama,

they aren't full of anything—not life
not grief, just stone polished

to a mirror, my face sliced
by the shadow of its wings.

SNAPDRAGONS (II)

The night before my third MRI I filched three
from a stalk in a stranger's garden, hoarded
their leafless heads beneath my pillow. For luck,
I told myself, but when I lifted my head no bloom
was whole: their cheeks unhinged, lips crushed. No thunder
or battering wings. Nothing but a cataclysm of petals,
my dragons' halved mouths rippling and red as marrow.

THE NIGHT BEFORE MY DIAGNOSIS IS CONFIRMED,

Mama enters the train's half-lit compartment,
slides in across from me. She looks like she did

in the old pictures, no bruises on her arms, full head
of hair. She says, *You rooted in me like a sickness*,
and recounts, again, the story of my birth.

How the doctors told her that her womb killed
everything, said, *Don't get too attached.*

How my father, still in love, found one
November rose on the new bush they'd planted
that year, and when he brought it to her with the eggs

she couldn't keep down, she said, *It's a girl.*

I curl up small as a sonogram and tell her
that the last rose I cut from that bush cradled
a nest of aphids big as my thumb.

The train rocks, its whistle knifing
the night. Her hands ripple

like a pair of torn wings. *They sliced
you out like a tumor*, she says. *Look,
the scar is shaped like a sickle.*

I say, *There's something wrong, Mama.
I feel teeth knocking in my heart.*

She doesn't look at me. Her lips
are blue as drowning.

She says, *I told you*
you were poison.

The windows buckle, fists of wind snatching
her hair. Around us, the rails are a clatter
of tuneless bells. My spit thickens

and I remember why she isn't here. Can't be.
Mama, you aren't supposed to be alive.

She's gone in a cloud of moth dust that sticks
to the roof of my mouth, gone except for the needle

of breath in my ear saying, *Daughter,*
neither are you.

IN TOULOUSE (II)

I haven't spoken in days

                    In the courtyard, crows gather
dusk's last light in their wings
                        I lift my head

                  they say the wind here cries
          itself mad and I imagine a lost girl
grieving through the streets at night

               If I swallowed that wind
would my tongue turn
        to the clapper of a bell

                Could I sing again?

HOW NOT TO REMEMBER YOUR MOTHER

The night I turned sixteen, Mama almost called an exorcist.
I'd been out with a friend who believed she was a witch. It was easier
to let Mama flick holy water into my eyes than to tell her

I'd been practicing a different kind of worship,
easier to let her die thinking I was straight.

I'm not supposed to remember her this way.
We're supposed to carry our dead
with reverence. I know. But I confess,

some days I like her better gone.

Like last April, when a cold front sheeted
my lilacs in ice, and I loved them that way,
loved them so much I didn't care that the afternoon thaw
would kill them, loved them enough

to say to nobody, *It's a good thing she died before I—*
and I shut my mouth with the force of a trap
snapping a mouse's neck.

Like the first time I let a strange man
fuck me. How I would've given anything to call her,
to say, *See, Mama, I didn't let you down. Please come back.*

MS NOCTURNE WITH FUSE, CROSSHAIRS, AND IRREPARABLE FISSURE

my brain's a dirty bomb

                a malcontent } a sycamore

lashed with lightning

                with lesions } my future

a series of losses

                scried on a readout } the atlas

my doctor makes

                of my body } fissuring

no promises

                my right eye } crosshaired

yet I cleave to

                yes } I can still feel

a needle skimming

                my foot sole } not numb yet

not puncturing

                if the insurance } holds out

just a needle and

                some pills } a few MRIs a year

not a fuse

                and if I'm careful } no detonation

DEAR BURGLAR,

You must have thought I was a junkie. Syringes everywhere.
Upturned biohazard box. My bed, thanks to you, a graveyard
of blunted needles. This is the second time you've turned me

over. I've stopped opening my blinds. I've doweled the window
you used so it won't yield anymore. Twice a night, I rouse myself
to double-check my locks. I prefer, despite statistics, to imagine you

as a woman, scrappy in your dark flannel, hair buzzed short,
like mine, lifting my TV through the back window with
a dancer's ease. I almost like you this way, rogue that you are.

I can begin to believe that you won't come back again. Listen,
among those things you took—vodka, knapsack, laptop—
in that red box lined in faux velvet, there was a pearl, a gift I gave,

once, to my mother. I remember how, in Hawai'i, the pearl stand
lady cracked three oysters before one relinquished its treasure.
Silver is for wisdom, she said, as it rolled between my heart-

and lifelines. There were few gifts my mother loved
like she loved that pearl. It hung from her neck every day
at the hospice center and from mine for a year after,

until I could no longer suffer its weight. Almost as heavy
was the pendant she'd given me after her lone pilgrimage
to the Vatican. Did you cradle that little portrait of Saint Francis

like I used to? Did you know his prayer begins, *Lord, make me an instrument of your peace. Where there is hatred let me sow love. Where there is injury, pardon*? Burglar, I'm no saint. I will not forgive you. But I have mercy enough

to be glad I had no MS drug for you to take, that night. Copaxone burns like brimstone even when you inject it properly, and you left the guidebook beneath my bed. How could you have known what you were doing?

LOVE POEM TO INJECTION-SITE REACTIONS

I would say *mottled* but that's not quite true.
Mottled is stormcloud, is sculpin, is pig iron.
You're more like *curdled*, if skin were capable

of spoiling—ridged and risen and birthday-balloon
red, never the same two days in a row.

My MS specialist says driving the needle
deeper will lessen the rippling sting of you
(unless I hit muscle; then you'll knell

through my arm for a week). She assures me
you'll vanish one day. A phase, like the spangly

cowgirl boots I outgrew when I was nine. For now,
we're stuck a few more years in this uneasy
marriage, but the truth is, I've grown to love you

a little. Every time I press the plunger down, you throb
brave, brave, brave, & I believe you. You're the proof.

ASKED IF I MISS MY MOTHER, I SAY I MISS THE HOUSE

Even if I never see it again, that house holds me.
Everywhere I wander, dropping a trail
of fingernails curved like swan necks—

Seven years and twelve addresses later, the lace
of mud I tracked on that carpet still looks like veins
in a bee's wing. The hardwood still hums

with hymns she sang odd hours, the plucked
strings of the harp I built but did not build
alone. The walls still ring with the warnings

of train whistles, the jar on my nightstand
still full of mashed pennies with their faces
rubbed off. Once, she strung them into wind

chimes, hung them over the porch. They didn't hold.
Ice shook them down, a hail of warped copper
crushing the snowdrops. That house is a dream

waiting for my head to nod, a labyrinth
doubling back on itself, tree rings missing
a center. I will follow the trail I made

until I stumble across the door—
I will nibble it down each day
as if it were made of bread.

MS NOCTURNE ACCORDING TO ECCLESIASTES

a time for sugar   and for drought

                                             for magic

          and the absence of magic

                                             a time

for slacked lips   for lemoned lips

                                                       for lips bitten

with iodine   a time

                              again

          for punctures limned

                                   in burning

for nimbuses

                    of antiseptic

a time to   skinflint sleep

               and cancel plans

                                        a time not

     to heal   (spinal nerve darkening

          on its bobbin)   & a time to praise

a body's wonder   not *despite*

     but *because*

LOVE POEM TO MYSELF

Sweet girl, you are less monster
than you think. Your spine,
notched with thistle and iron,

silvers with magic, with *yes*.
Lovely, you are not the names
your mother called you, not

the halfmoon bruise on your hip,
the note that blisters sharp
from your pennywhistle.

When you linger so long
near the knife block it asks
for your blood, I am with you.

Emily, I give you back
your name, shuttered
like honeysuckle between

the bindings of your books.
That's how much I love you.
Don't forget.

WHAT I DIDN'T CALL HER

Not Mama, not when
she was alive.

I like the sound of it now,
like she was someone

I could've called *Mama*,
not *Mother*, like I did

since I was twelve. My parents
were *Mother* and *Daddy*

so even strangers would know
which one I liked better,

which one liked *me* better.
I had so few weapons,

but this was a dart
I could launch over

and over, as if this small
formality could say,

I stopped loving you
before you stopped loving me.

I never knew how deeply
it gored her until the first time

I said *Mom* in the sickroom
and my godmother recognized

the whip of white flag
in my voice, asked me

if I called her *Mom* now,
squeezed my wrist, said,

That's huge, I'm so glad.
So it was *Mom* for six

more months, and *Mama*
in every poem I've written
since then, because
I wish we could have

been like that. I wish
I couldn't only say it now

because there's no harm
in it for either of us.

ACKNOWLEDGMENTS

The poems "Self-Portrait as Judy Garland," "Self-Portrait as Persephone Returning," "Self-Portrait as Dorothy Gale," and "Portrait: Mama as Demeter" appear in the chapbook Love & a Loaded Gun, released in 2017 by Minerva Rising Press, under slightly different titles.

Many thanks to the editors of the following publications where some of these poems have appeared, sometimes under different titles:

Academy of American Poets Website—"Premonition" (reprinted from *Spoon River Poetry Review*, winner, 2015 Academy of American Poets Prize)

American Life in Poetry—"What Makes a Pearl" (reprinted from *The Minnesota Review*)

The Arkansas International—"Nocturne with Witch & Desire"

Atticus Review—"Love Poem to Injection-Site Reactions" (third place winner of the *Atticus Review*'s poetry contest)

BOAAT Journal—"All I Wanted" (finalist, 2016 Orlando Prize)

The Boiler Journal—"In Toulouse (i)" and "In Toulouse (ii)"

Carve Magazine—"MS Nocturne According to Ecclesiastes"

december magazine—"The night before my diagnosis is confirmed" (finalist, Jeff Marks Poetry Prize, Spring 2017)

The Doubleback Review—"Lent"

IthacaLit—"Self-Portrait as Dorothy Gale" (honorable mention, 2016 Difficult Fruit Prize)

Jabberwock Review—"Self-Portrait as Judy Garland" (as "Judy Garland Speaks of Her Early Career," winner, 2014 Nancy D. Hargrove Editor's Prize)

Luna Luna Magazine—"Protection Spell" (as "Spell for Protection")

The Mid-American Review—"Spell for the Fissured Brain," "Spell for Courage," and "Spell for the Grief Song Scarred to Your Throat" (finalist, 2017 Fineline Prize)

The Minnesota Review—"What Makes a Pearl"

Nimrod—"Asked If I Miss My Mother, I Say I Miss the House" (finalist, 2015 Pablo Neruda Prize; finalist, *Yemassee*'s 2015 Pocataligo Poetry Prize)

Orison Anthology—"MRI, Barnes Jewish Hospital" (winner, 2017 Orison Anthology Award)

Philadelphia Stories—"Self-Portrait as Rapunzel" (winner, 2014 Sandy Crimmins Award)

Phoebe—"MS Nocturne without a Magician" (finalist, 2017 Greg Grummer Prize)

The Pinch—"Self-Portrait as Persephone Returning" and "What I Didn't Call Her" ("Self-Portrait as Persephone Returning" was a featured poem in 2017)

Raleigh Review—"How Not to Remember Your Mother" (finalist, 2017 Laux/Millar Prize)

Rust + Moth—"Portrait: Mama as Demeter"

Salamander—"Dear Burglar"

Smartish Pace—"Snapdragons (i)" and "Snapdragons (ii)" (finalist, 2016 Beullah Rose Prize)

So to Speak—"After the Transplant Fails, I Dream of Crocodiles" (finalist, 2016 Poetry Contest)

South Carolina Review—"Love Poem to Myself"

Southern Indiana Review—"At Her Funeral, Singing"

Spoon River Poetry Review—"Premonition" (honorable mention, 2015 SRPR Editor's Prize)

Sweet—"MS Nocturne with Fuse, Crosshairs, and Irreparable Fissure" (runner up, 2019 Poetry Competition)

The Superstition Review—"Love Poem to Risk," "Another Premonition" (as "In Toulouse (i)"), and "At Cimetière de Terre Cabade"

Sycamore Review—"Her Cancer into Harvest" (finalist, 2016 Wabash Poetry Prize)

Tinderbox Poetry Journal—"In the Year of the Divorce, My Fascinations Include: Surrealism, the Dust Bowl, and *The Wizard of Oz*," "Four Poisons," and "Passport" (finalists, 2016 Tinderbox Poetry Prize; "In the Year . . ." was a finalist for the 2016 Fairy Tale Review Award)

Tupelo Quarterly—"Still Life with Lines from Isaiah"

Vitamin ZZZ, Clinical Issue—"MS Nocturne without a Magician" (reprinted from *Phoebe*)

Waccamaw—"Double Memory with Train"

Washington Square Review—"Hospice"

Yemassee—"Prayer"

Some of these poems also appear in the following anthologies: *The Familiar Wild: On Dogs and Poetry* ("Lovebites"), *Fiolet and Wing: An Anthology of Domestic Fabulist Poetry* ("Self-Portrait as Judy Garland"), *Bramble & Thorn Anthology* ("Prayer"), *Philadelphia Stories' 15th Anniversary Anthology* ("Self-Portrait as Rapunzel"), and *Drought: The Absence of Something Specified* ("Self-Portrait as Rapunzel").

Deep gratitude to my teachers, including Judith Sornberger, Louise Sullivan-Blum, and Teri Doerksen at Mansfield University; Judy Jordan, Allison Joseph, Pinckney Benedict, Jennifer Key, and the sorely missed Jon Tribble at Southern Illinois University Carbondale; and Rebecca Lindenberg and John Drury at the University of Cincinnati.

Thank you to my writer pals at Southern Illinois University Carbondale and at the University of Cincinnati, including (but not limited to) Seanse Ducken, Molly Bess Rector, Dan Paul, Brett Gaffney, Brenda Johnson, Micah Dean Hicks, Brenda Peynado, Molly Brayman, Rochelle Hurt, Corey van Landingham, Emily Skaja, Sarah Rose Nordgren, Kelly Pieper, Madeleine Wattenberg, Chelsea Whitton, Yalie Kamara, Marianne Chan, Matthew Yeager, Kimberley Grey, Johnathan Travelstead, Jacqueline Zhang, Kirk Schuleter, Jessica Suchon, Josh Myers, Sequoia Nagamatsu, Cole Nagamatsu, Austin Allen, Caitlin Doyle, David Fairbanks, Alyssha Nelson, Lathan Ehlers, Andy Harper, Leila Chatti, Avery Guess, Meghann Plunkett, Anna Knowles, Ruth Awad, Teresa Dzieglewicz, Andrew Hemmert, John McCarthy, Lucien Meadows, Robert Parrott, Laura Ruffino, and especially Toni Judnitch, the world's most extraordinary roommate. You and so many of my other dear friends have shaped me as a poet and a person.

Thanks not just to my parents, Cliff Cole and Pam West, but to the whole, huge network of Coles, Wests, Zapps, and Showalters who have bolstered me throughout the years with creativity, encouragement, and kindness. I love all of you.

Wisconsin Poetry Series

Edited by Ronald Wallace and Sean Bishop

How the End First Showed (B) • D. M. Aderibigbe

New Jersey (B) • Betsy Andrews

Salt (B) • Renée Ashley

Horizon Note (B) • Robin Behn

About Crows (FP) • Craig Blais

Mrs. Dumpty (FP) • Chana Bloch

The Declarable Future (4L) • Jennifer Boyden

The Mouths of Grazing Things (B) • Jennifer Boyden

Help Is on the Way (4L) • John Brehm

No Day at the Beach • John Brehm

Sea of Faith (B) • John Brehm

Reunion (FP) • Fleda Brown

Brief Landing on the Earth's Surface (B) • Juanita Brunk

Ejo: Poems, Rwanda, 1991–1994 (FP) • Derick Burleson

Jagged with Love (B) • Susanna Childress

Almost Nothing to Be Scared Of (4L) • David Clewell

The Low End of Higher Things • David Clewell

Now We're Getting Somewhere (FP) • David Clewell

Taken Somehow by Surprise (4L) • David Clewell

Thunderhead • Emily Rose Cole

Borrowed Dress (FP) • Cathy Colman

Dear Terror, Dear Splendor • Melissa Crowe

Places/Everyone (B) • Jim Daniels

Show and Tell • Jim Daniels

Darkroom (B) • Jazzy Danziger

And Her Soul Out of Nothing (B) • Olena Kalytiak Davis

My Favorite Tyrants (B) • Joanne Diaz

Talking to Strangers (B) • Patricia Dobler

Alien Miss • Carlina Duan

(B) = Winner of the Brittingham Prize in Poetry

(FP) = Winner of the Felix Pollak Prize in Poetry

(4L) = Winner of the Four Lakes Prize in Poetry